TICKET TO THE FINAL FOUR

MARTIN GITLIN

ADMIT ONE

THE BIG GAME

YOUR FRONT ROW SEAT

45th Parallel Press

Published in the United States of America by Cherry Lake Publishing Group
Ann Arbor, Michigan
www.cherrylakepublishing.com

Reading Adviser: Beth Walker Gambro, MS Ed., Reading Consultant, Yorkville, IL.

Photo Credits: © AP Photo/David J. Phillip, cover; © jira pliankharom/Shutterstock, inside cover, 13, 19, 25; © Nosyrevy/Shutterstock, 2, 3, 6, 9, 10, 16, 23, 32; © Pierre E. Debbas/Shutterstock, 5; © AP Photo/Morry Gash/ASSOCIATED PRESS, 7; Public Domain via Wikimedia Commons, 9 (top), 9 (bottom); Public Domain, University of California Library via Internet Archive, 11; John Mac, CC BY-SA 2.0 via Wikimedia Commons, 12; © AP Photo/File/ASSOCIATED PRESS, 15; © AP Photo/File/ASSOCIATED PRESS, 17; © John Hanson Pye/Shutterstock, 18; © Alayna Stevens/The Reflector, 21; © Alayna Stevens/The Reflector, 22; Chairman of the Joint Chiefs of Staff, CC BY 2.0 via Wikimedia Commons, 24; © Photo by John Jones/Icon Sportswire/ASSOCIATED PRESS, 27; © Yuri Arcurs/Dreamstime.com , 28; © lrkhamster stock/Shutterstock, 29

45th Parallel Press is an imprint of Cherry Lake Publishing Group.

Library of Congress Cataloging-in-Publication Data

Names: Gitlin, Marty, author.
Title: Ticket to the Final Four / by Martin Gitlin.
Other titles: Final Four
Description: Ann Arbor, Michigan : 45th Parallel Press, [2025] | Series: The big game | ATOS: 4.00 (w/in the 3rd grade ATOS band) | Includes bibliographical references. | Audience: Grades 7-9 | Summary: "Who has won the Final Four? How did they make it happen? Filled with high-interest text written with struggling readers in mind, this series includes fun facts, intriguing stories, and captivating play-by-plays from the final four games of NCAA's March Madness"-- Provided by publisher.
Identifiers: LCCN 2025009418 | ISBN 9781668963869 (hardcover) | ISBN 9781668965184 (paperback) | ISBN 9781668966792 (ebook) | ISBN 9781668968406 (pdf)
Subjects: LCSH: NCAA Basketball Tournament--History--Juvenile literature. | National Collegiate Athletic Association--Juvenile literature. | National Association of Intercollegiate Athletics--Juvenile literature. | Basketball--Tournaments--United States--History--Juvenile literature. | College sports--United States--History--Juvenile literature.
Classification: LCC GV885.49.N37 G58 2025 | DDC 796.323/630973--dc23/eng/20250429
LC record available at https://lccn.loc.gov/2025009418

Cherry Lake Publishing Group would like to acknowledge the work of the Partnership for 21st Century Learning, a Network of Battelle for Kids. Please visit Battelle for Kids online for more information.

Printed in the United States of America

Table of Contents

Introduction

The NCAA organizes college sports. The NCAA is the National Collegiate Athletic Association. It sets the rules. It ranks teams. Basketball is one of its biggest sports. Players work to be NCAA champs.

March Madness is college basketball at its finest. It features the best men's and women's teams in the country. There is nothing like it.

March Madness starts in March. It ends in April. It begins with 68 teams. They play game after game. The losers drop out. The winners advance to the next round. March Madness is exciting. It is for the **championship**. That is the event that decides the NCAA winner.

The waiting is over and the big game is about to begin! Get ready, college basketball fans!

After the first 2 rounds, 16 teams are left. These are the Sweet 16. The winners move on. They become the Elite 8.

Then it happens. Only 4 teams remain. They are the best of the best. They are the Final Four. The games are played in huge arenas. There are no empty seats. Every ticket is sold.

The Final Four begins with 2 games. The 2 winners compete for the title. The title game is played 2 days later. And when it ends, the NCAA champion is crowned.

Let the big games begin!

The Iowa Hawkeyes and University of South Carolina Gamecocks battled in the 2024 NCAA Finals.

History of the Game

Harold Olsen was the Ohio State men's basketball coach. He had an idea in 1939. Olsen wanted to start a **tournament**. That is a series of games played to determine a champion. So he organized one.

The event started small. It began with 8 teams. Each was picked from a different area of the country. It was a success. His team reached the finals. Then they lost to Oregon.

The phrase "March Madness" may have been **coined** that same year. Coined means invented. But it wasn't about college basketball. It was about high school basketball.

Oregon won the very first NCAA tournament.

1946 photograph of Ohio State Coach Harold Olsen

High School basketball was popular. Fans looked forward to tournaments. They were exciting. Henry Porter was a high school coach. He coached in Illinois. He wrote about that excitement. He said a "little March madness" could be a good thing.

The college tournament continued with 8 teams. Then a dispute arose in 1950. Both the University of North Carolina and the University of Kentucky earned spots. But they were both in the same area of the country. So the tournament expanded to 16 teams.

More teams meant more madness. The tournament expanded to 32 teams in 1975. It reached 64 in 1985. Four more were added by 2011.

March Madness excited fans. Especially when it reached the Final Four. Nobody could predict the winner. It seemed to change every year. There has only been one **dynasty**. That is a team that wins year after year. It was the University of California, Los Angeles (UCLA). The UCLA Bruins won 9 of 10 titles. That was from 1964 to 1973.

The UCLA Bruins won the 1973 NCAA tournament.

The Final Four was just for men for a long time. That changed in 1982. Women's basketball became more popular. More colleges had teams. The NCAA started a tournament for them.

Few called it March Madness. Crowds for the women's games were small. But they didn't stay small. Women's games became more competitive. Players grew in talent. Fans started paying attention.

Women's March Madness got huge in 2024. Great players drove up TV ratings. Fans packed arenas. More people watched the women's Final Four than the men's event.

Caitlin Clark brought excitement to the Final Four in 2024.

March Madness teams are divided into **seeds**. That is how they are ranked. It is based on their chances of winning the tournament.

Lower seeds usually lose early. They have to play the best teams from the start. But sometimes they pull an **upset**. That is when a team is expected to lose, but wins.. And that allows them to keep going.

Few low seeds make it far. But it has happened. The Villanova Wildcats were an eighth seed in 1985. Yet they took the championship that year.

Other lower seeds have almost won. Six No. 11 seeds have reached the Final Four. The earliest to do it was Louisiana State (LSU). That team made it in 1986. The most recent was North Carolina State in 2024.

! A BIT OF TRIVIA

Early Days, Big Moments

A **rivalry** can make games more exciting. A rivalry is a history of competition. There are 2 kinds of rivalries. One is between 2 teams. They have a history of exciting and close games. The other is between 2 players. They are usually the best talents. Their battles become epic.

It was 1979. Magic Johnson played for the Michigan State Spartans. Larry Bird played for the Indiana State Sycamores. March Madness began. Both teams continued to win. They reached the Final Four. Then they faced each other in the championship game. It had more TV viewers than any college basketball game ever. Both performed great. But Johnson played better. And the Spartans took the crown.

Magic Johnson and Larry Bird were rivals. But they still showed good sportsmanship. Bird helped Johnson up during the 1979 NCAA final game.

This was the beginning of their rivalry. They became **professional athletes**. Those are athletes paid to play. Their teams battled. Fans watched and cheered. They were fierce players. They also became great friends.

Bird and Johnson played for great teams. No one knew who would win. But March Madness often has upsets. That is when teams win when they are expected to lose. It has even happened in the Final Four.

One example was 1983. Fans thought the Houston Cougars would win it all. They had the best player in college basketball. His name was Hakeem Olajuwon. The Cougars were supposed to beat the North Carolina State Wolfpack.

The battle came down to the end. The score was tied at 52–52. Only a few seconds remained in the game. North Carolina State player Dereck Whittenburg heaved a 30-foot (9.1 meter) shot toward the basket. It missed.

But teammate Lorenzo Charles caught it. He slammed it through the hoop. The Wolfpack had upset Houston. They were the champions.

Charles's dunk that won the game for the Wolfpack

It doesn't take an upset to make history. Sheryl Swoopes did it by being the best. Swoopes is a legend. She is one of the greatest players in history.

Some might not have known her in 1993. But they would not forget her after that. Swoopes played for the Texas Tech Red Raiders. That team was playing for its first title. Its opponent was Ohio State.

Swoopes scored more than half her team's points. It was a close game. The Raiders won it, 84–82. And Swoopes dominated. She scored 47 points. That was a record. It was among the best Final Four performances ever.

Swoopes went on to star as a prefessional athlete.

Texas Tech's sports mascot is named Raider Red.

WAY BACK WHEN

Basketball was still largely **segregated** in 1966. That means separated by race. Black and White players usually played for different schools. Those with all Black players did not often compete in March Madness.

Then along came the Texas Western Miners. Their coach was Don Haskins. They had an all-Black team. And they were incredible. They won 28 of 29 games.

Their most notable opponent was Kentucky. Kentucky had an all-White team. In 1966, they played for the national title. The game received great attention. And the Miners won.

That victory had a big impact on college basketball. It led to more **integration**. That is when people are not separated by race.

Modern Moments

The University of Connecticut Huskies started a streak of women's basketball wins in 2014. They won championship after championship.

The Huskies did not lose for 3 years. Their win streak reached 111 games. It was the longest win streak in college basketball history.

They were about to win the 2017 title. The Huskies were in the Final Four. Their opponent was the Mississippi State Bulldogs. Few expected the Bulldogs to win.

Mississippi State had a player named Morgan William. She was shorter than average. But she had a big heart and big talent.

Bulldog Dominique Dillingham (00) blocks UConn player Crystal Dangerfield (5). The Huskies didn't expect what happened in this game.

Morgan William used her talent to win for Mississippi State.

The Bulldogs were tougher than most thought. The team surprised Connecticut. The Huskies were not used to playing close games. But there were just a few seconds left. And the score was tied 64–64.

William was just 5-foot-5 (165.1 centimeters). She could not shoot over anyone. But she was quick. William dribbled the ball downcourt. A Huskies player tried to stay with her. William then cut right. And she lofted a shot toward the basket.

Swish! The ball dropped through the hoop. Then time ran out. The Bulldogs had won. It was perhaps the biggest upset in women's college basketball history. A mob scene followed on the court. The Bulldogs enjoyed their big celebration.

Men's college basketball had a big rivalry moment in 2022. University of North Carolina's Tar Heels and the Duke University Blue Devils are rivals. Both teams are from North Carolina. The rivalry began in 1920. But it was in the spotlight in 2022.

Mike Krzyzewski coached at Duke for 42 seasons.

The rivals met in the Final Four. Duke coach Mike Krzyzewski was a legend. He coached Duke for 42 years. They won 5 national titles. They made it to 13 Final Fours. That was a record. And he was about to retire after the 2022 tournament. That made this game even more special.

The game was close. But the University of North Carolina emerged with the victory. Krzyzewski would not win a title in his last year. The Tar Heels made sure of it. He was done. But he would never be forgotten.

His name was Lew Alcindor. He later changed it to Kareem Abdul-Jabbar. He is 7-foot-2 (218.4 cm). And he was an incredible college basketball player.

Abdul-Jabbar played for the UCLA Bruins. He dominated in the late 1960s. His main weapon was the “sky hook.” That was a hook shot over defenders. Nobody could block it.

The Bruins dominated during his time there. They won 88 games and lost just 2. UCLA won all 3 national championships in a row with Abdul-Jabbar.

Abdul-Jabbar scored at least 24 points a game every season. Abdul-Jabbar also averaged at least 15 rebounds. He then grew into an NBA superstar. Abdul-Jabbar is one of the greatest players ever.

LEGEND OF THE SPORT

Rising Stars

College basketball stars often play just one season. Then they go pro. They become professional players. The rising stars are high school players. Colleges track their play. They **recruit** the best of the best. Recruit means ask to join.

A. J. Dybantsa

Dybantsa graduated high school in 2025. But he's already a star. Dybantsa scored 19 points a game as a freshman. He averaged 9.6 rebounds a game. As a senior, he averaged 21.2 points and 9.4 rebounds a game.

The young star wasted little time making a big decision. He decided to stay in Utah for college basketball. Dybantsa signed to play at Brigham Young University. That school is getting a possible superstar.

Utah's Dybantsa, who was already a star in high school

Aaliyah Chavez

Aaliyah Chavez was one of the best high school scorers ever. Chavez played at Monterey High School. That is in Texas. She placed that school in the spotlight. Chavez averaged 38 points per game as a junior. That is amazing.

Then she kept scoring. Chavez began her senior year averaging 35 points a game. In one game, she scored 53. Chavez added 46 in another. She decided to play for Oklahoma University in 2025.

Chavez is definitely a star on the rise.

Stars like Aaliyah Chavez score big for their teams. They know they can't win games alone.

It was the 2016 men's championship game. The University of North Carolina Tar Heels were trying to win it all. Their opponents were the Villanova University Wildcats.

The excitement was at a fever pitch. Villanova led 74–71. Only 7 seconds remained in the game. Tar Heels player Marcus Paige attempted a 3-point shot. And it went in. That tied the game at 74–74.

Villanova got the ball back. Ryan Arcidiacono passed it to Kris Jenkins. Jenkins shot the ball from the right side of the court. It arced high in the air. It seemed like it took forever to come down. But the ball landed through the net.

It was over. The Villanova Wildcats had won the championship. They celebrated as gold and white confetti streamed down on them. They would cherish that moment forever.

AMAZING MOMENT

Activity

March Madness brackets are popular. They are also fun. They are how people predict who will win March Madness games. It tracks games from the beginning to the end of the event. Folks even predict the champion.

Get a sturdy poster board. Draw a blank March Madness bracket. Examples can be found online. Place all the first-round March Madness matchups on it. Then study the teams. Which are the best? Which teams do you believe will win the first round? Then go through every game in every round. Predict every winning team through the Final Four and championship game.

Don't stop there. Ask your friends to predict all the games on your bracket. Maybe family members will also want to play. This activity might make it more fun to watch the games. When the Final Four is over, look at everyone's predictions. Who did the best? Did anyone correctly pick the champion?

Learn More

BOOKS

Barnes, Derrick D. *Basketball: Amazing but True Stories!* New York, NY: Workman, 2023.

Gitlin, Martin. *Taming the Huskies.* Ann Arbor, MI: Cherry Lake Publishing, 2024.

WEBSITES

Search these online sources with an adult.

Sports Illustrated for Kids: March Madness

NCAA | What is March Madness: The NCAA tournament explained

Glossary

championship (CHAM-pee-uhn-ship) event that determines the winner in a league or sport

coined (KOYND) invented or created, such as a word or phrase

dynasty (DIYE-nuh-stee) team that wins championships year after year

integration (in-tuh-GRAY-shuhn) bringing together people from different groups (like race) into one group

professional athletes (pruh-FESH-nuhl ATH-leets) athletes who are paid to play

recruit (rih-KROOT) to ask or convince to join

rivalry (RIYE-vuhl-ree) relationship between teams or players with a history of competition

seeds (SEEDZ) team rankings based on chances to win a tournament

segregation (seh-grih-GAY-shuhn) separation of people based on race

tournament (TUR-nuh-muhnt) event in which a series of games is played to determine a champion

upset (UP-set) game won by a team expected to lose

Index

About the Author

Martin Gitlin is an educational book author based in Connecticut. He won more than 45 awards as a newspaper sportswriter from 1991 to 2002. Included was a first-place award from the Associated Press for his coverage of the 1995 World Series. He has had more than 200 books published since 2006. Most of them were written for students.